JumpStart Your Growth

Books by Dr. John C. Maxwell
Can Teach You How to Be a REAL Success

Relationships

25 Ways to Win with People

Becoming a Person of Influence

Encouragement Changes Everything

Ethics 101

Everyone Communicates, Few Connect

The Power of Partnership

Relationships 101

Winning With People

Equipping

The 15 Invaluable Laws of Growth

The 17 Essential Qualities of a Team Player

The 17 Indisputable Laws of Teamwork

Developing the Leaders Around You

Equipping 101

Learning from the Giants

Make Today Count

Mentoring 101

My Dream Map

Partners in Prayer

Put Your Dream to the Test

Running with the Giants

Talent Is Never Enough

Today Matters

Wisdom from Women in the Bible

Your Road Map for Success

Attitude

Attitude 101

The Difference Maker

Failing Forward

How Successful People Think

How Successful People Win

Sometimes You Win, Sometimes You Learn

Success 101

Thinking for a Change

The Winning Attitude

Leadership

The 10th Anniversary Edition of The 21 Irrefutable Laws of Leadership

The 21 Indispensable Qualities of a Leader

The 21 Most Powerful Minutes in a Leader's Day

The 360 Degree Leader

Developing the Leader Within You

The 5 Levels of Leadership

Go for Gold

JumpStart Your Leadership

Leadership 101

Leadership Gold

Leadership Promises for Every Day

A 90-DAY
IMPROVEMENT
PLAN

JumpStart Your Growth

JOHN C. MAXWELL

CENTER
STREET

NEW YORK   BOSTON   NASHVILLE

The author is represented by Yates & Yates, LLP,
Literary Agency, Orange, California.

Literary development and design: Koechel Peterson & Associates, Inc., Minneapolis, Minnesota.

This book has been adapted from *The 15 Invaluable Laws of Growth*, copyright © 2012 by John C. Maxwell. Published by Center Street.

Center Street
Hachette Book Group
1290 Avenue of the Americas
New York, NY 10104

www.CenterStreet.com

Printed in the United States of America

RRD-C

First trade edition: August 2015
10 9 8 7 6 5 4 3 2 1

Center Street is a division of Hachette Book Group, Inc.
The Center Street name and logo are trademarks of Hachette Book Group, Inc.

The Hachette Speakers Bureau provides a wide range of authors for speaking events. To find out more, go to www.hachettespeakersbureau.com or call (866) 376-6591.

The publisher is not responsible for websites (or their content) that are not owned by the publisher.

ISBN 978-1-4555-8831-2

INTRODUCTION

Since you are reading these words, no doubt you want to be a better person tomorrow than you are today. You want to grow in some way. Perhaps you want to progress in your career, live a healthier lifestyle, increase your knowledge, have a stronger relationship with someone, deepen your spiritual life, or achieve a lifelong dream.

I believe you can achieve it. You have so much potential inside of you. But do you currently have the tools to do so? Do you know how to get better at what you do? To improve your relationships? To reach your goals? How do you gain more depth and wisdom as a person? How do you overcome obstacles? Should you work harder, work longer, wait for things to get better?

The answer is that you need to have an intentional, strategic plan for growth.

Many people learn from the school of hard knocks. Difficult experiences teach them random lessons "the hard way," and they change—sometimes for better, sometimes for worse.

You have dreams, goals, and aspirations. Do you assume that if you just work really hard you'll improve naturally? I once believed that. Then I discovered that personal growth doesn't just happen on its own. We have to be strategic about it. We need to take complete ownership of our growth process, because nobody else will do it for us. If we want our lives to improve, we must improve ourselves.

This book is my effort to help you learn how to grow and develop yourself so you have the best chance of becoming the person you were created to be. Intentional growth is the key that will unlock the door to your potential. Over the next 90 days, you will be provided with clear steps to help you become a more effective and fulfilled individual. No matter where you are in your growth journey or what challenges you face, you have a chance to improve yourself through personal growth from this day forward.

What will it take for you to get started? Consistently set aside 15 minutes every day for the next 90 days to grow intentionally. Read and think about the inspirational quote for the day, read and digest the lesson, and move forward by taking action in response to the question.

If you spend time growing on purpose every day for the next three months, you will be on your way to reaching your potential. You will make intentional growth a habit. And you will look back and be astounded by how far you've come.

Ready? Let's get started!

DAY

1

A time comes when you need to stop waiting for the man you want to become and start being the man you want to be.
BRUCE SPRINGSTEEN

Potential is one of the most wonderful words in any language. It looks forward with optimism. It is filled with hope. It promises success. It implies fulfillment. It hints at greatness. Potential is a word based on possibilities. Think about your potential as a human being and you get excited—at least, I hope you do. What a positive thought. I believe in your potential just as much as I believe in mine. Do you have potential? Absolutely.

Since you are reading these words, I believe you have the desire to jumpstart your growth so you can reach your potential. My question to you is, "Do you have a plan for your personal growth?" I was asked that question when I was in my twenties and it changed my life. I believe it can change yours as well. When I started my career, I was intentional about working, reaching my goals, and being successful. I had a strategy: hard work. I hoped that would get me where I wanted to go, but hope isn't a strategy and working hard doesn't guarantee success. I realized I did not have a plan.

So do you have a plan for how you can become all you can be?

Describe what you believe about your potential, and then describe how you have hoped or planned to become all you can be.

DAY

2

*Life lived for tomorrow will always be
a day away from being realized.*
LEO BUSCAGLIA

If you're like I was, you have one or more mistaken beliefs that create a gap that keeps you from growing and reaching your potential. Misconceptions about growth, such as thinking that by simply working hard that we will automatically grow, will hold you back from being as intentional as you need to be. Or we assume that although we really don't know how to grow, someone in our world will have a plan for improving us. When I was seeking answers, not one person I asked had figured this out.

Perhaps you're holding back because of fear or you're looking for the "best" way to get started in a growth plan. Granted, growing involves admitting you don't have the answers, and it requires that you get over any fear you may have of making mistakes or looking foolish. And I found that I had to get started if I wanted to find the best way. That is the price of admission if you want to improve. To become intentional about growing, expect to make mistakes every day, starting today, and welcome them as a sign that you are moving in the right direction.

List the beliefs that have been holding you back from starting in a growth plan. What truths can you use to overcome these misconceptions and jumpstart the growth process?

DAY

3

Motivation is not going to strike you like lightning. . . .
The whole idea of motivation is a trap.
Forget motivation. Just do it.
JENNIFER REED

Another misconception gap that may be keeping you from growing and reaching your potential is that you think you need to feel inspired to learn and grow. When I realized I needed to be intentional about growing, I didn't have the time, the money, or the experience to do it. I only had the hope that it would make a difference. That didn't feel inspired, but I started anyway. To my astonishment, after a year of dedicated growth, I started to pass some of my heroes. It made a huge difference. After that, I didn't want to miss a single day!

If you're having difficulty finding inspiration to continue, please trust me when I say that the reasons to *keep* growing far outweigh the reasons that led you to *start* growing. And you discover the reasons to stay with growth only if you stick with it long enough to start reaping the benefits. So make a commitment to yourself to stick with it for at least twelve months. If you do, you will fall in love with the process, and you will be able to look back at the end of that year and be amazed at how far you've come.

Have you allowed a lack of feeling to hold you back? Write out your personal declaration of commitment to growth, sign and date it. Then stick with it for at least ninety days and be amazed.

DAY

4

The only way you learn is to surround yourself
with people who are better than you.
MICKEY SUMNER

Fairly early in my career, I attended an idea exchange with three other people whose organizations were six times the size of mine, and they had many more and much better ideas than I did. I went because at the time I realized that if my goal was to be a better leader, I needed to be exposed to bigger and better leaders outside of my own small circle.

At first when I arrived, I was intimidated. As we talked and shared ideas, it became clear very quickly that I was not in their league. I felt like I was in over my head and trying to swim. Despite that, I was encouraged, because I discovered that great men were willing to share their ideas and I was learning so much.

For the first ten years that I was intentionally pursuing personal growth, I had to get over the comparison gap, because I felt like I was always behind and trying to catch up. I had to learn to become comfortable with being out of my comfort zone, and so will you. It can be a difficult transition, but you can learn *only* if others are ahead of you, which makes it well worth the discomfort.

Where can you meet other people in the area you want to grow? Do you know the people you need to help you already? Do some research. Is there a conference where you can connect with and learn from other like-minded people?

DAY

5

You are the same person today that you are going to be in five years from now except for two things: the people with whom you associate and the books you read.
CHARLES "TREMENDOUS" JONES

According to research by social psychologist Dr. David McClelland of Harvard, the people with whom you habitually associate are called your "reference group," and these people determine as much as 95 percent of your success or failure in life. And Jim Rohn asserted that we become the combined average of the five people we hang around the most.

It is always profitable to associate with people "larger" than ourselves. We should try to spend our time with people with integrity. People who are positive. People who are ahead of us professionally. People who lift us up instead of knocking us down. People who take the high road, never the low. And above all, people who are growing.

You cannot take the growth journey alone, not if you want to reach your potential. The most significant factor in any person's environment is the people. If you change nothing else in your life for the better than that, you will have increased your chances of success tenfold. So think long and hard about whom you're spending the most time with, for wherever they are headed, so are you.

Make a list of the people who are currently most influential in your life. What will you do to increase the influence of those who are "larger" than you and can stretch you?

DAY

6

You cannot change your destination overnight,
but you can change your direction overnight.
JIM ROHN

The first year that I engaged in intentional personal growth, I soon discovered that it was going to be a lifetime process. During that year, the question in my mind changed from "How long will this take?" to "How far can I go?" That is the question you should be asking yourself right now—not that you will be able to answer it. I started this growth journey forty years ago, and I still haven't answered it. But it will help you set the direction, if not the distance.

The best you can hope to do in life is to make the most out of whatever you've been given. You do that by investing in yourself, making yourself the best you can be. The more you've got to work with, the greater your potential—and the farther you should try to go. Give growing your best so you can become your best.

Where do you want to go in life? What direction do you want to go? What's the farthest you can imagine going?

DAY

7

Can there be a more insidious word? "Later," as in "I'll do it later." . . the diet that starts "tomorrow," the job hunt that happens "eventually," the pursuit of the life dream that begins "someday" combine with other self-imposed roadblocks and lock us on autopilot.

JENNIFER REED

When I was still in my 20s, I heard businessman and philanthropist W. Clement Stone speak on the idea of having a sense of urgency. His seminar session was titled "Do It Now," and one of the things he told us was this: "Before you get out of bed every morning, say 'do it now' fifty times. At the end of the day before you go to sleep, the last thing you should do is say 'do it now' fifty times." In that moment it felt like he was talking to me personally. I went home, and for the next six months I did exactly that. It gave me a tremendous sense of urgency.

The greatest danger you face in this moment is the belief that you can make intentional growth a priority *later*. Don't fall into that trap! By starting to read this book, you've already begun the process. Don't stop there! Keep taking more steps. Pick a resource that will help you grow and begin learning from it *today*.

Write the words "Do It Now!" somewhere where you will see them every day. Then the next time you are considering waiting to take action, repeat the phrase and actually DO IT NOW. Write about the results.

DAY

8

Feed your fears and your faith will starve.
Feed your faith, and your fears will.
MAX LUCADO

Growing can be a messy business that requires courage. I recently read an article on the fears that keep people from being successful. The following five factors came into play:

Fear of failure
Fear of trading security for the unknown
Fear of being overextended financially
Fear of what others will say or think
Fear that success will alienate peers

Which of those fears most impacts you? For me it was the last one: alienating my peers. By nature I'm a people pleaser, and I wanted everyone to like me. It really doesn't matter which fear affects you the most. We all have fears. But here's the good news. We also all have faith. The question you have to ask yourself is, "Which emotion will I allow to be stronger?" Your answer is important, because the stronger emotion wins. I want to encourage you to feed your faith and starve your fear.

*Which of
the five fears
creates the
greatest barrier
to your intent
to grow? Why?
Describe how
you will feed
your faith
and starve
your fear to
overcome it.*

DAY

*One's philosophy is not best expressed in words;
it is expressed in the choices one makes. In the long run,
we shape our lives and we shape ourselves.*

ELEANOR ROOSEVELT

Perhaps at this stage you're realizing you've been stuck in the rut of accidental growth, where you just experience life and hope that you learn what you need along the way merely from experience. But this is keeping you from the solid track of intentional growth. The following comparison should help bring clarity about the difference:

Accidental Growth	*Intentional Growth*
Plans to start tomorrow	Insists on starting today
Waits for growth to come	Takes complete responsibility to grow
Learns only from mistakes	Often learns before mistakes
Depends on good luck	Relies on hard work
Quits early and often	Perseveres long and hard
Falls into bad habits	Fights for good habits
Talks big	Follows through
Plays it safe	Takes risks
Thinks like a victim	Thinks like a learner
Relies on talent	Relies on character
Stops learning after graduation	Never stops growing

Identify the one attitude in the left column that is the greatest obstacle to your growth and use the idea in the right column to help you change by taking action to overcome it. Write out how you will do it.

DAY

10

The first step toward change is awareness.
The second step is acceptance.
NATHANIEL BRANDEN

If you want to grow, you must know yourself: your strengths and weaknesses, your interests and opportunities. You must be able to gauge not only where you've been, but also where you are now. Otherwise you cannot set a course for where you want to go. And of course, every time you want to learn something, you must be able to take the new thing you've learned today and build upon what you learned yesterday to keep growing. That's the only way to gain traction and keep improving yourself.

Most people don't know what they would like to do. They don't know themselves as well as they should, and thus remain unfocused in their growth. What makes finding themselves and growing to their potential difficult for some people is that it can be a bit of a catch-22. You have to know who you are to grow to your potential. But you have to grow in order to know who you are. So what's the solution?

Explore yourself as you explore growth. The way to start is to pay attention to your passions. That awareness is a must to knowing yourself, and when you accept who you are, you can focus on your passions and start building.

How well do you know yourself? List your interests, strengths, weaknesses, opportunities, and passions. Then focus in on your passions. Where do you want them to take you in life?

....

....

....

....

....

....

....

....

....

....

....

....

....

....

....

....

....

....

....

DAY

11

If, as Socrates said, the unexamined life is not worth living,
so the unlived life is worth examining.
ABRAHAM KAPLAN

I am amazed by how many people I meet every day who don't like doing what they do for a living. Why do they do it? I understand the necessity of having to make a living. I've done jobs I didn't like. But I didn't stay there my whole life, doing something I found unfulfilling. If I'd loved it and it had fit my passion and purpose, I would have tried to build a career there. But it wasn't what I wanted to do.

If you're not enjoying what you do for a living, take some time to examine why. Is it a risk making a change from what you're currently doing to what you want to do? Of course. You might fail. You might find out that you don't like it as much as you expected. You might not make as much money. But isn't there also great risk in staying where you are? You might fail, get fired, or take a pay cut anyway. Or worst of all, you might come to the end of your life feeling regret for never having reached your potential or doing what you love. Which risk would you rather live with?

Do you like the work you are doing now? Why? List the ways that it does—and doesn't—fit with your passions and purpose.

DAY

12

*Every successful person I've met has a strong
sense of his or her unique abilities and aspirations.
They're leaders in their own lives, and they dare to
pursue their dreams on their own terms.*

MARIA BARTIROMO

There is definitely a direct connection between finding your passion and reaching your potential. So have you found and harnessed your passion? Do you know what you would like to do? When you do, it makes all the difference. Why? When you tap into your passion, it gives you the E&E factor: energy and excellence. Nothing's work unless you'd rather be doing something else. Passion gives you an advantage over others, because one person with passion is greater than ninety-nine who have only an interest!

People say there are two great days in a person's life: the day you were born and the day you discover why. Author Stephen Covey observed, "How different our lives are when we really know what is deeply important to us, and keeping that picture in mind, we manage ourselves each day to be and to know what matter's most."

Knowing yourself and what you want to do is one of the most important things you'll ever do in this life. I want to encourage you to seek what you were put on this earth to do. Then pursue it with all your effort.

What would you like to be doing? Write down the things that are deeply important to you. How can you see yourself contributing in those areas? Explore what you believe you might have been put on this earth to do.

DAY

13

Discover your uniqueness;
then discipline yourself to develop it.
JIM SUNDBERG

One of the main keys to being successful and fulfilling your purpose is to understand your unique talents and to find the right arena in which to use them. There's a big difference between having a dream that propels you to achieve and pulling an idea out of thin air that has no connection with who you are and what you can do. You must have some kind of criteria for knowing if the desire you have matches the abilities you possess.

Warren Bennis offers three questions you can ask yourself to identify if what you want to do is possible:

Do you know the difference between what you want and what you're good at?

Do you know what drives you and what gives you satisfaction?

Do you know what your values and priorities are, and what your organization's values and priorities are?

Measuring those three differences reveals many of the obstacles between you and what you want to do. At that point the question you need to ask yourself is whether you are able to overcome those differences.

What talents, skills, experience, and opportunities do you possess that support your desire to do what you want to do?

DAY

14

Your vision will become clear only when you look into your heart. Who looks outside, dreams. Who looks inside, awakens.

CARL JUNG

It's very important not only to know what you want to do, but also why you want to do it. I say that because motives matter. When you do things for the right reason, which would be to make a positive difference in the lives of others, it gives you inner strength when things go wrong. Unselfish motives help you to build positive relationships because they prevent hidden agendas and incline you to put people ahead of your agenda. Doing something for the right reasons also keeps life less cluttered and your path clearer. Not only is your vision clearer, but you also sleep well at night knowing you're on the right track.

The work that I do is a calling on my life. When I lead or communicate, I think, *I was born for this*. It relies on my strengths. It gives me energy. More importantly, it makes a difference in the lives of others. That fulfills me and gives me a touch of the eternal.

I believe you can have the same kind of satisfaction and can experience success if you do the things you were meant to do, and do them for the right reasons. Take time to reflect. Explore your intentions and attitudes. As you know yourself, you will grow yourself.

What are your motives for doing what you would like to do? Ask yourself, "Why do I want to do this?" Examine your intentions.

DAY

15

If you want to get from where you are to where you want to be, you have to start by becoming aware of the choices that lead you away from your desired destination. Become very conscious of every choice you make today so you can begin to make smarter choices moving forward.

Darren Hardy

To move from what you're doing now to what you want to do is a process. I believe it begins with . . .

Awareness. Spend some time really thinking about where you're presently headed. If it's not where you want to go, write out what steps you need to take to go where you desire to go, to do what you want to do.

Action. You cannot win if you do not begin! It means doing something specific every day that will take you another step closer to your goal.

Accountability. Few things prompt a person to follow through like accountability. Request that specific individuals ask you about your progress. Write down every action that pertains to an area (finances, health, career, or relationships) where you want to see improvement.

Attraction. If you're growing, you attract others who are growing. This puts you in a position to begin building a community of like-minded people who can help one another succeed.

What steps must you take (beginning today) in the areas of awareness, action, accountability, and attractions, to move closer to doing what you want to do?

DAY

16

A mentor is someone who sees more talent and ability within you, than you see in yourself, and helps bring it out of you.
BOB PROCTOR

My greatest growth has always come as a result of finding people ahead of me who were able to show me the way forward. Some of them have helped me through personal contact, but most have helped through the wisdom I've found in the books they've written.

If you have discovered what you want to do, start finding people who do that with excellence. Then do what you must to learn from them . . .

Get committed. Pay people for their time if necessary.

Be consistent. Meet purposefully every month with someone who can teach you.

Be creative. Start with their books if you can't meet them in person.

Be purposeful. Spend two hours in preparation for every hour of interaction.

Be reflective. Spend two hours in reflection for every hour of interaction.

Be grateful. These people are gifts to your personal growth; be sure to let them know.

Always remember that you will need the help of others to guide you on your way.

Think of three people who do what you want to do with excellence. What will you do today to start learning from them?

DAY

17

Probably the most honest self-made man ever was the one we heard say: "I got to the top the hard way—fighting my own laziness and ignorance every step of the way."

JAMES THOM

Because I have the privilege of doing what I've always wanted to do, I want to help you see ahead to what that's like. First, it will be *different* from what you imagined. I never thought that I would affect as many people as I do. I never knew life would be so beautiful. But I also never anticipated the expectations others would put on me to produce.

When you do what you want to do, it will be *more difficult* than you ever imagined. I had no idea how much time it would take to be effective. I never expected to have to keep paying the price to be successful. I also never dreamed that my energy level would be affected as much as it has in recent years.

Finally, let me tell you this. When you do what you've always wanted to, it will be *better* than you ever imagined. When I started investing in my personal growth, I didn't anticipate a compounding return—for me personally, for the individuals I've mentored, and for my team. And I never dreamed it would be this much fun! Nothing else compares to doing what you were created to do.

Picture yourself being successful. What do you imagine will be required of you to achieve that success? How will it be rewarding?

DAY

18

No factor is more important in people's psychological development and motivation than the value judgments they make about themselves. Every aspect of their lives is impacted by the way they see themselves.

NATHANIEL BRANDEN

I often ask myself why so many people fail to grow and reach their potential. I've concluded that one of the main reasons is low self-esteem. Many people don't believe in themselves. They don't see the possibilities they were born with. They possess a hundred acres of possibilities, yet never cultivate them because they are convinced that they won't be able to learn and grow and blossom into something wonderful.

Often I heard my friend Zig Ziglar say, "It's impossible to consistently behave in a manner inconsistent with how we see ourselves. We can do very few things in a positive way if we feel negative about ourselves." You can't outperform your self-image. If you don't realize that you have genuine value and that you are worth investing in, you will never put in the time and effort needed to grow to your potential. It is a lid on your potential. If you want to become the person you have the potential to be, you must believe you can—no matter what anyone else believes or says!

Make a list of all of your best personal qualities. Using the list as a springboard, decide on the one word that best describes you. How will you make this word your North Star as you begin adding value to yourself?

DAY

19

*By the time you're seventeen years old, you've heard
"No, you can't," an average of 150,000 times. You've heard
"Yes, you can," about 5,000 times. That's thirty nos for
every yes. That makes for a powerful belief of "I can't."*
JOHN ASSARAF AND MURRAY SMITH

Whether you realize it or not, you have a running conversation with yourself all the time. What is the nature of yours? Do you encourage or criticize yourself? If you are positive, you help to create a positive self-image. If you're negative, you undermine your self-worth. Where does negative, critical self-talk come from? Usually from our upbringing.

If you want to change your life, you have to change the way you think of yourself. If you want to change the way you think of yourself, you need to change the way you talk to yourself. You need to learn to become your own encourager. Every time you do a good job, don't just let it pass; give yourself a compliment. Every time you choose discipline over indulgence, don't tell yourself that you should have anyway; recognize how much you are helping yourself. Every time you make a mistake, don't bring up everything that's wrong with yourself; tell yourself that you're paying the price for growth and that you will learn to do better next time. Every positive thing you can say to yourself will help.

What is the nature of your self-talk? Write a list of the positive and negative thoughts you have about yourself. Tally the number of times you think something positive or negative about yourself over the next 24 hours.

DAY

*Don't compare yourself with anyone in this world . . .
if you do so, you are insulting yourself.*
BILL GATES

When I started my career, I looked forward to the annual report from the organization showing statistics for each of its leaders. As soon as I received it, I'd look for my standing and compare my progress with the progress of all the other leaders. After about five years of doing that, I realized how harmful it was.

What happens when you compare yourself to others? Usually it's one of two things: either you perceive the other person to be far ahead of you and you feel discouraged, or you perceive yourself to be better than the other person, and you become proud. Neither of those is good for you, and neither will help you to grow.

Comparing yourself to others is really just a needless distraction. The only one you should compare yourself to is you. Your mission is to become better today than you were yesterday. You do that by focusing on what you can do today to improve and grow. Do that enough, and if you look back and compare the you of weeks, months, or years ago to the you of today, you should be greatly encouraged by your progress.

Who do you compare yourself to? How do you feel when you do that? Change your focus by writing one way in which you have improved yourself.

DAY

21

*When a man has put a limit on what he will do,
he has put a limit on what he can do.*

CHARLES SCHWAB

Most people are like the comic character Shoe, who says in one of my favorite comic strips, "When it comes to believing in myself, I'm an agnostic." The greatest limitations people experience on their lives are usually the ones they impose upon themselves.

Author Jack Canfield offers a solution to self-limiting thinking. In his book *The Success Principles*, he recommends the following four steps to transform limiting beliefs into empowering beliefs:

1. *Identify a limiting belief that you want to change.*
2. *Determine how the belief limits you.*
3. *Decide how you want to be, act, or feel.*
4. *Create a turnaround statement that affirms or gives you permission to be, act, or feel this new way.*

That's really good advice. Once you do it, repeat that turnaround statement to yourself every day for as long as you must in order to change your self-limiting thinking. Remember, in the end, it isn't what you are that holds you back; it's what you think you're not.

Identify a limiting belief that you want to change. Create a turnaround statement that affirms or gives you permission to he, act, or feel a new way.

DAY

Act as if what you do makes a difference. It does.
WILLIAM JAMES

Because people with low self-esteem often see themselves as inadequate or feel like victims, they focus inordinately on themselves. They can become self-protective and selfish because they feel that they have to be to survive.

If that is true of you, then you can combat those feelings by serving others and working to add value to them. Making a difference—even a small one—in the lives of other people lifts one's self-esteem. It's hard to feel bad about yourself when you're doing something good for someone else. In addition to that, adding value to others makes them value you more. It creates a cycle of positive feeling from one person to another.

It is also the right thing to do, and one of the best ways to build self-esteem is to do what's right, to be true to yourself and your values. It gives a strong sense of satisfaction. Every time you take action that builds your character, you become stronger as a person—the harder the task, the greater the character builder. You can actually "act yourself" into feeling good about yourself, because positive character expands into every area of your life, giving you confidence and positive feelings about everything you do.

How much time every week do you spend focusing on others and adding value to them? What step will you take to serve others on a weekly basis?

DAY

23

The first step is you have to say that you can.
WILL SMITH

If there is an area in your life that seems overwhelming to you—health, work, family, or something else—try chipping away at it a little bit every day instead of trying to tackle it all at once. Since your self-worth is based upon the positive habits, actions, and decisions you practice every day, why not build your self-esteem and tackle your biggest problems at the same time? Don't fret or worry about it; do something specific about it. Discipline is a morale builder. Boost yours by taking small steps that will take you in a positive direction.

And when you do the right thing or you take a small step in the right direction, take a break and celebrate the small victories. If nothing is ever good enough, you can lose heart. Celebrating encourages you. It helps to inspire you to keep going. Tell yourself, "I did the right thing—good for me! I'm that much closer to success." Don't underestimate the power of small victory celebrations. Every positive action you take helps you to believe in yourself, which in turn helps you to take more positive action.

List three small growth steps you will take today in a positive direction and how you will celebrate the victories.

DAY

24

Personal development is the belief that you are worth the effort, time, and energy needed to develop yourself.
DENIS WAITLEY

What do you value? What prompts you to see a positive vision for your life? If you don't have a vision, you are likely to be apathetic. However, if you tap into what you value and try to see what could be, it can inspire you to take positive action.

I wish I could sit down with you, hear your story, and encourage you specifically in your journey. If you've had a difficult time and you don't feel good about yourself, I want to tell you that you do have value. You matter. Your life can change, and you can make a difference—no matter what kind of background you have or where you come from. No matter what traumas you've suffered or mistakes you've made, you can learn and grow. You can become the person you have the potential to be. You just need to believe in yourself. And every time you take a step, think a positive thought, make a good choice, or practice a small discipline, you're moving one step closer. Just keep moving forward, and keep believing.

Describe your vision for your life. What do you dream of becoming? What is the next step you will take to keep moving forward toward that dream?

DAY

25

Follow effective action with quiet reflection. From the quiet reflection will come even more effective action.
PETER F. DRUCKER

If you're nearly as old as I am, you may remember an old slogan once used by Coca-Cola. They called Coke "the pause that refreshes." Well, reflection is the pause that helps someone to grow. Learning to pause allows growth to catch up with you.

For at least the last two thousand years, people have been quoting Julius Caesar as saying that experience is the best teacher. With all due respect to Caesar, I have to disagree. Experience is not the best teacher. Evaluated experience is! The only reason anyone was able to make that claim was because he had learned much by reflecting on his life and writing about it.

There's an old joke that experience is a hard teacher because the test is given first and the lesson is given afterward. That's true, but only if the person takes time to reflect after the experience. Otherwise, you receive the test first and the lesson may never come. People have innumerable experiences every day, and many learn nothing from them because they never take the time to pause and reflect. That's why it is so important to pause and let understanding catch up with us.

Take out your calendar and schedule time to pause and reflect for ten to thirty minutes at the end of every day, at least an hour or two every week, part of a day several times a year, and as little as a day and as much as a week annually. Guard this time as you would your most important appointments.

DAY

26

*Life can only be understood backwards;
but it must be lived forwards.*
SØREN KIERKEGAARD

Stopping to pause and reflect is one of the most valuable activities people can do to grow. It has much greater value to them than even motivation or encouragement. Why? Because pausing allows them to make sure they are on the right track. After all, if someone is going down the wrong road, he doesn't need motivation to speed up. He needs to stop, reflect, and change course.

If we don't take the time to pause and reflect, we can miss the significance of certain experiences that are life markers. We go to a place or are part of an event or meet a person that in some way marks us for life because something important happened. Often these markers identify a time of transition, change, or transformation. Reflection allows these life *markers* to become life *makers*. If we pause to allow growth to catch up with us, it makes our lives better, because we not only better understand the significance of what we've experienced, but we can implement changes and course corrections as a result. We are also better equipped to teach others from the wisdom we have gained.

Pause and write out your reflection on the last significant person or experience that changed the way you think. How has that become or how can it become a life maker?

....
....
....
....
....
....
....
....

....
....
....
....
....
....
....
....
....
....

DAY

27

When you are able to create a lonely place in the middle of your actions and concerns, your successes and failures slowly can lose some of their power over you.
HENRI J. M. NOUWEN

Study the lives of the great people who have made an impact on the world, and you will find that in virtually every case, they spent a considerable amount of time alone thinking. Every significant religious leader in history spent time in solitude. Every political leader who had an impact on history practiced the discipline of solitude to think and plan. Great artists spend countless hours in their studios or with their instruments not just doing, but exploring their ideas and experiences. Most leading universities give their faculty time not only to teach, but also to think, research, and write.

Time alone allows people to sort through their experience, put it into perspective, and plan for the future.

I strongly encourage you to find a place to think and to discipline yourself to pause and use it, because it has the potential to change your life. It might be a room in your home, a quiet public place, or even your car. Wherever it is, it can help you to figure out what's really important and what isn't.

What will work practically for you? Identify two or three places where you can consistently and effectively pause and reflect. Then go to one to think.

DAY

28

All truths are easy to understand once they are discovered.
The point is to discover them. That takes investigation.

GALILEO

When you take the time to pause and reflect, these are the basic directions your thinking should go:

Investigation. Pausing means more than just slowing down to smell the roses. It means stopping and really figuring things out. That generally requires a person to ask questions. Continual growth from experiences is only possible when we discover insights and truths within them through investigation.

Incubation. This means taking an experience of life and putting it into the slow cooker of your mind to simmer for a while. It is very similar to meditation—listening and learning. I give ideas as long as they need until I discover an insight or experience the next "I," which is . . .

Illumination. Jim Rohn remarked, "At the end of each day, you should play back the tapes of your performance. The results should either applaud you or prod you." What he's talking about is illumination. These are the "aha" moments in your life, the epiphanies when you experience sudden realization or insight. It's when the proverbial lightbulb turns on. Few things in life are more rewarding than such moments.

At the end of this day, pause and reflect on your performance. Write down the insights and truths you discover. What illumination do you gather from the day?

DAY

29

Successful people ask better questions,
and as a result, they get better answers.
ANTHONY ROBBINS

Whenever I take time to pause and reflect, I begin by asking myself a question. Whenever I'm thinking and reflecting and I feel like I've hit a roadblock, I ask myself questions. If I'm trying to learn something new or delve deeper into an area so I can grow, I ask questions. I spend a lot of my life asking questions.

I cannot overemphasize the importance of asking good questions when it comes to personal growth. If your questions are focused, they will stimulate creative thinking. Why? Because there is something about a well-worded question that often penetrates to the heart of the matter and triggers new ideas and insights.

If your questions are honest, they will lead to solid convictions. If you ask quality questions, they will help you to create a high-quality life. Sir Francis Bacon—English philosopher, statesman, scientist, lawyer, jurist, author, and pioneer of the scientific method—asserted, "If a person will begin with certainties, he will end in doubts; but if he will be content to begin with doubts, he will end in certainties."

Where do you most need to grow right now? Write a list of questions to help you examine and assess what you need to do to make that happen. If you're having trouble getting started, try these words: What, Why, How, When, Who.

DAY

30

*What we do on some great occasion
will depend on what we are; and what we are will be
the result of previous years of self-discipline.*
H. P. LIDDON

What you want to accomplish in life and where you are in the journey will determine what areas you most need to think about today, and the questions you must ask yourself have to be tailored to your situation. But the most important thing you must do is write out the questions that help you develop personal awareness, and then write out the answers. Why? Because you will discover that what you think after you write the answer is different from what you thought before you wrote it. Writing helps you to discover what you truly know, think, and believe.

All of this probably sounds like a lot of work. You're right; it is. That's why most people never do it. But it is worth every bit of the effort you put into it. The farther you go in life, the more critical it is that you take time to pause and think. Never forget that your goal in personal growth is reaching your potential. Here's the good news: If you've been diligent in your efforts to grow along the way, you will also be better equipped to fulfill that purpose, even if it requires you to make significant changes or course corrections.

Yesterday you wrote out a list of questions to help you examine and assess what you need to do to grow right now. Now write out the answers to those questions.

DAY

31

The hallmark of excellence, the test of greatness, is consistency.
JIM TRESSEL

I'm a big believer in motivation and encouragement. But here's the truth when it comes to personal growth: Motivation gets you going, but discipline keeps you growing. It doesn't matter how talented you are or how many opportunities you receive. If you want to grow, consistency is key. If you want to become more disciplined and consistent in your performance, you need to become more disciplined and consistent in your growth.

I sometimes see people who know their purpose yet are inconsistent in their progress. They have the ambition to succeed and they show aptitude for their job, yet they do not move forward. Why? Because they think they can master their job and don't need to master themselves. What a mistake.

Your future is dependent upon your personal growth. Improving yourself daily guarantees you a future filled with possibilities. When you expand yourself, you expand your horizons, your options, your opportunities, your potential. The more tuned in you are to your purpose, and the more dedicated you are to growing toward it, the better your chances of reaching your potential, expanding your possibilities, and doing something significant.

Name one thing you'd like to improve about yourself. Make a plan to do one thing every day for the next week that will help you improve in that area and follow that plan.

DAY

Problems arise for the introverts because they often do not look closely enough at the outer situation and, therefore, do not really see it. The extraverts often do not stop looking at the specific situation long enough to see the underlying idea.

ISABEL BRIGGS MYERS

Do you have a handle on how to improve yourself? To become consistent in your growth, start by leveraging your personality type to get yourself going. If you tap into the strength in your personality type, you will set yourself up for success when it comes to motivation.

If you are phlegmatic, you tend to be easygoing and likeable but may lack initiative. To motivate yourself, you need to find the value in what you need to do and focus on it.

If you are choleric, you take charge easily and make decisions quickly, but you tend to not participate when you're not "in charge." You will find motivation by taking charge of how you will grow and sticking with it.

If you are sanguine, you tend to be fun-loving but may often lack focus. To motivate yourself to grow, make a game of it or give yourself rewards for incremental successes.

If you are melancholic, you are attentive to detail, but your desire for perfection may tend to make you afraid of making mistakes. To motivate yourself, focus on the joy of developing a level of mastery over your subject matter.

Take a personality profile quiz to help you determine your personality type. (Examples include Myers-Briggs Type Indicator, DiSC, and Personality Plus.) Write a description of how you can align your methods of motivation with your personality type.

DAY

33

*I work on the same principle as people who train horses.
You start with low fences, easily achieved goals, and work
up. It's important in management never to ask people
to try to accomplish goals they can't accept.*
IAN MACGREGOR

What is the number one mistake of first-time gardeners? The same as that of many people who approach personal growth for the first time: attempting too much. What is the result? Discouragement. When you attempt too much too soon, you're almost guaranteed to fall short of your desired results. That is demotivating. The secret to building motivational momentum is to start small with the simple stuff.

If you want to gain momentum and improve your motivation, begin by setting goals that are worthwhile but highly achievable. Master the basics. Then practice them every day without fail. Small disciplines repeated with consistency every day lead to great achievements gained slowly over time.

Andrew Wood asserted, "Where many people go wrong in trying to reach their goals is in constantly looking for the big hit, the home run, the magic answer that suddenly transforms their dreams into reality. The problem is that the big hit never comes without a great deal of little hits first. Success in most things comes not from some gigantic stroke of fate, but from simple, incremental progress."

Write a list of the five simple, incremental steps you will take to reach a goal in your personal growth. Can you achieve step 1 today?

DAY

34

Have patience. All things are difficult before they become easy.
SAADI

When I give someone advice to be patient, I must admit that I am the person who most needs to take it. Impatience is one of my greatest weaknesses. I think it comes from having unrealistic expectations—for myself and others. Everything I want to do takes longer than I anticipate. Every endeavor I lead is more difficult than I believed it would be. Every project I attempt costs more than I expected. Every task I hand off to another person is more complicated than I hoped. Some days I believe that patience is a minor form of despair disguised as a virtue.

I'm not alone in this. If you're an American, as I am, you may agree that as a culture, we have a problem with patience. We want everything fast. We live in a country with fast-food restaurants and fast-weight-loss clinics. How ironic.

Most people never realize how close they are to achieving significant things, because they give up too soon. Everything worthwhile in life takes dedication and time. The people who grow and achieve the most are the ones who harness the power of patience and persistence.

In what areas do you consider yourself an impatient person? What can you do to become more patient in these areas?

DAY

35

Too many people believe that one big, public success will solve their self-confidence problems forever. That only happens in the movies. In real life, the opposite strategy is what works. Call it the "small victories" approach.
JACK AND SUZY WELCH

One of the best things you can do for yourself as a learner is to cultivate the ability to value and enjoy the process of growth. It is going to take a long time, so you might as well enjoy the journey.

Years ago, my friend Charlene Armitage, who is a successful life coach, highlighted the importance of the process that people must develop in order to grow and change the direction of their lives. She said, "Life goals are reached by setting annual goals. Annual goals are reached by reaching daily goals. Daily goals are reached by doing things that may be uncomfortable at first but eventually become habits. Habits are powerful things. Habits turn actions into attitudes, and attitudes into lifestyles."

You can visualize tomorrow using it as motivation to grow, but if you want to actually grow, your focus needs to be on today. If you value today and find a way to enjoy the process, you will invest in today. And the small steps you take today will lead to the bigger steps you take someday.

What habits or activities do you enjoy that also help you grow personally? Schedule time today to pursue these habits.

DAY

36

Once you learn to quit it becomes a habit.
VINCE LOMBARDI

Knowing *what* to improve and *how* to improve are critical to consistency in personal growth. But so is knowing *why*. The *how* and *what* will take you only so far. The *why* is what keeps you motivated long after that first rush of energy and enthusiasm wears off. Having a strong *why* will help you to keep going when the discipline of learning becomes difficult, discouraging, or tedious. If your growth is connected to your values, dreams, and purpose, you'll know why you're doing it. It can carry you through when willpower isn't enough. Think of it as *why*-power.

You have to give yourself more and bigger *why*s so you can keep wanting to put in the effort to grow. The more valid reasons you have to achieve your dream, the higher the odds are that you will. That principle is also true of growth. The greater number of reasons you give yourself to grow, the more likely you will be to follow through.

When you make the right choices—however small— and do it consistently over time, it can make a huge difference in your life. If you remember *why* you're making those choices, it becomes easier.

Compile your list of "whys" for pursuing personal growth, noting immediate benefits as well as long-term ones. Feel free to add to this list whenever you discover a new reason.

DAY

37

From the time you get up in the morning to the time you go to sleep at night, your habits largely control the words you say, the things you do, and the ways you react and respond.

BRIAN TRACY

When do you need to improve? First the obvious answer: right now. Today. More important, you need today to be every day.

You will never change your life until you change something you do daily. That means developing great habits. Discipline is the bridge between goals and accomplishments, and that bridge must be crossed every day. Over time that daily crossing becomes a habit. And ultimately, people do not decide their future; they decide their habits and their habits decide their future.

What are you doing daily that needs to change? What needs doing? Maybe more important, what needs undoing? Advice columnist Abigail Van Buren quipped, "A bad habit never goes away by itself. It's always an undo-it-yourself project." What are you willing to change doing today in order to change what you will be doing tomorrow?

A week ago, on Day 30, you made a plan to do something toward a goal each day. Did you follow through? Think about your experience is that plan working or do you need to do something differently?

DAY

38

It's not what we do once in a while that shapes our lives.
It's what we do consistently.
ANTHONY ROBBINS

Consistency isn't easy, but to be successful we must learn to become consistent. You must figure out what works for you, but here's what has worked for me. Instead of being goal conscious, I focus on being growth conscious. Here's the difference:

<u>Goal Consciousness</u>	<u>Growth Consciousness</u>
Focuses on a destination	Focuses on the journey
Motivates you and others	Matures you and others
Seasonal	Lifelong
Challenges you	Changes you
Stops when a goal is reached	Keeps you growing beyond the goal

I am such a strong believer in people and in human potential that I don't ever want to put a lid on it by setting goals that are too small. If you can believe in yourself and the potential that is in you, and then focus on growth instead of goals, there's no telling how far you can grow. You just need to consistently put in the work as you keep believing in yourself.

In what ways do you tend to focus on goals rather than growth? What might you do to shift your focus more toward growth consciousness?

DAY

39

There are two primary choices in life: to accept conditions as they exist, or accept the responsibility for changing them.
DENIS WAITLEY

When I first realized I needed to grow, I sat down and penned what I call "My Growth Environment." It has helped to guide my decisions concerning personal growth since then. It says, in a growth environment . . .

Others are *Ahead of me.*
I am continually *Challenged.*
My focus is *Forward.*
The atmosphere is *Affirming.*
Failure is not my *Enemy.*
I wake up *Excited.*

I am often out of my *Comfort Zone.*
Others are *Growing.*
People desire *Change.*
Growth is *Modeled* and *Expected.*

When my intuition was telling me that my environment wasn't conducive to personal growth, I went back to that list and found that most of those statements did not apply to my current situation. So I determined to change myself and change my environment. If you read that list and you sensed that most of those statements do not apply to your life, you may need to do the same thing.

Assess your current environment by answering true or false to each of the ten statements about a growth environment. If you answer false to more than five of the statements, your current environment may be hampering your growth.

DAY

40

The first step toward success is taken when you refuse to be a captive of the environment you first find yourself in.
MARK CAINE

I believe at some point during every person's lifetime, there comes a need to change environments in order to grow to reach our potential, because we must be in the right environment. That usually requires us to make changes in our life.

You've probably seen the phrase *growth = change*. It's possible to change without growing, but it's impossible to grow without changing. One of the keys to making the right changes that allow us to grow is knowing the difference between a problem or challenge, which we can change, and a fact of life, which we cannot. For example, you cannot change who your parents are, your height or face, or your DNA. But you can change your attitude about them. You must do your best to live with them.

A problem is different. A problem is something you can do something about. If your current environment is negative, you can change it—or at least begin making small changes leading up to leaving it.

Write an honest review of whether your present work environment is a place where you believe you will thrive and grow. If it is an obstacle to growth, what will you do to change it?

DAY

41

Love yourself enough to create an environment in your life that is conducive to the nourishment of your personal growth. Allow yourself to let go of the people, thoughts, and situations that poison your well-being.

STEVE MARABOLI

If you are considering making a change from one professional environment to another more growth-conducive environment, you must make sure it's the right one. In my transitions, I started by spending a good amount of time assessing where I was and why I wanted to change. Those main reasons were enough to make me look at the uncomfortable truth of needing to make changes.

One of the ways to judge whether you're growing and in a growth-conducive environment is to discern whether you're looking forward to what you're doing. If the future looks dull or confining, start looking to make changes.

If you find it difficult to make that judgment about your situation, you can approach it from another direction. Ask yourself questions to help you understand who and what nurtures you personally, and then figure out whether or not you're getting those things. The main idea is to know yourself and to assess whether you're getting what you need in your current environment. If you are, celebrate. If you're not, prepare yourself to make some hard choices.

In your present professional environment, describe who or what nurtures you personally. What does the future look like to you?

DAY

42

Walk with the wise and become wise,
for a companion of fools suffers harm.
KING SOLOMON

Many years ago, I met author Elmer Towns, whose books I admired. During a private conversation, he asked me, "Do you know how to get a fireplace poker hot? Put it next to the fire." He then went on to explain that if our environment is cold, we're cold. If it's hot, we're hot. "If you want to grow," he said, "then spend time with great people; visit great places; attend great events; read great books, listen to great tapes."

Those words sent me on my quest to meet with leaders around the country who were ahead of me professionally. It changed my life.

If changing environments isn't a viable option to you, get closer to people who fire you up. Their heat, in the form of passion, talent, energy, vision, and enthusiasm, will spread to you and help you keep growing and learning no matter what obstacles you face.

Whose red-hot fire do you admire? What can you do to spend some time learning from them?

DAY

43

*The secret of success is to be ready
when your opportunity comes.*
BENJAMIN DISRAELI

One of the most positive things about being in a growth environment is that it gives you room to fly, but you must seize the growth opportunities you have and develop the habit and discipline of challenging yourself.

One of the first ways that I challenged myself was by making my goals public. Few things push a person like a deadline and an audience. Another way I've challenged myself is to look for one major growth opportunity every week, follow through on it, and learn from it. If it involves meeting with someone who is ahead of me, I prepare by asking five questions ahead of time:

What are their strengths? (to learn the most)

What are they learning now? (to catch their passion)

What do I need right now? (to apply what I learn to my situation)

Who have they met, what have they read, or what have they done that has helped them? (to find additional growth opportunities)

What haven't I asked that I should have? (to enable them to point out changes I need to make from their perspective)

Schedule a time to meet with at least one person who is ahead of you in an area of growth in the next week. Plan for the meeting by asking yourself the five questions I ask myself.

DAY

44

Do what you can, where you are, with what you have.
THEODORE ROOSEVELT

The changes we want to make in our lives come only in the present. Mother Teresa observed, "Yesterday is gone. Tomorrow has not yet come. We have only today. Let us begin." If you need to make changes in yourself and your environment, don't dwell on your past. You can't change it. Don't worry about your future. You can't control it. Focus on the current moment and what you can do now.

Growth always comes from taking action, and taking action almost always brings criticism. Poet Ralph Waldo Emerson observed, "Whatever course you decide upon, there is always someone to tell you that you are wrong." Their words may hurt, but move forward anyway. To reach your potential, you must do not only what others believe you cannot do, but also what even you believe you cannot do. Most people underestimate themselves. They shoot for what they know they can reach. Instead they should reach for what's beyond their grasp. If you don't try to create the future you want, you must endure the future you get.

Think of one of your personal growth goals. What do you think you are capable of achieving in that area? Now think one level beyond that, and take action toward reaching it.

DAY

45

If you don't design your own life plan, chances are you'll fall into someone else's plan. And guess what they may have planned for you? Not much.

JIM ROHN

Most people allow their lives to simply happen to them. They float along. They wait. They react. And by the time a large portion of their life is behind them, they realize they should have been more proactive and strategic. They allowed their lives to become complicated and entrusted their plans to others.

I believe life is pretty simple. It's a matter of knowing your values, making some key decisions based on those values, and then managing those decisions on a day-to-day basis. But life has a way of becoming complicated, and it is only through great effort that we can keep it simple.

From a conversation with Neil Cole, I came away with a determination to design my life as simply as possible by discovering and developing systems for growth that can be (1) received personally, (2) repeated easily, and (3) transferred strategically. Those systems help me fight the battle against complexity in my life every day. I believe they can help you too—if you can take action. A beautifully conceived strategy does you no good if you can't use it.

Write an honest review of the strategies you have developed for growth. What do you need to change in any of them to make them personal, repeatable, and transferable?

DAY

46

You only live once. But if you work it right, once is enough.
FRED ALLEN

There is no warm-up for life, no dress rehearsal, yet that's the way many people seem to be treating it. Each of us goes on stage cold, with no preparation, and we have to figure it out as we go along. That can be messy. We fail. We make mistakes. But we still need to give it our best from the very start.

If you plan your life well, your career will work itself out. The problem is that most people don't spend very much time planning their careers either. They spend more time planning for Christmas or their vacation. Why? Because people focus on what they think will give them the greatest return. If you don't believe you can succeed in your life in the long term, you're not very likely to give it the planning attention it deserves.

Planning your life is about finding yourself, knowing who you are, and then customizing a design for your growth. Once you draw the blueprint for your life, you can apply it to your career.

Write an assessment of which areas in your life receive the most of your strategic planning time (career, faith, family, health, hobby, marriage, personal growth, vacation). What areas need to become a higher priority?

DAY

47

Be not afraid of growing slowly;
be afraid only of standing still.
CHINESE PROVERB

I'm aware that I'm an impatient person, but I think all people naturally desire for things to come to them quickly and easily, including personal growth. Over the course of time, I've learned that the important things in life usually take longer than we expect and cost more than we anticipate. The secret isn't really to want more or want it faster. It's to put more time and attention into what you have and what you can do now.

Give three times the effort and energy to growing yourself. And allow yourself to grow slowly and with deep roots. Remember that a squash vine or tomato plant grows in a matter of weeks, produces for several days or weeks, and then dies when the first frost comes. In comparison, a tree grows slowly—over years, decades, or even centuries; it produces fruit for decades; and if healthy, it stands up to frost, storms, and drought.

As you develop strategies for growth, give yourself the time and resources you need. Whatever amounts seem reasonable to you, multiply them by two. That practice will help to keep you from becoming discouraged and giving up too soon.

Write a list of the areas of your growth that are taking longer or costing more than you anticipated. What change can you make to your growth strategy to keep you moving forward?

DAY

48

Systems permit ordinary people to achieve extraordinary results predictably. However, without a system, even extraordinary people find it difficult to predictably achieve even ordinary results.
MICHAEL GERBER

Most accomplishments in life come more easily if you approach them strategically. Rarely does a haphazard approach to anything succeed, and if it does, it's not repeatable. So how do you accomplish something strategically on a consistent basis? By creating and using systems. One of the greatest keys to my personal growth and high productivity is that I use systems for everything.

What is a system? It's a process for predictably achieving a goal based on specific, orderly, repeatable principles and practices. Systems leverage your time, money, and abilities. They are great tools for personal growth. Systems are deliberate, intentional, and practical. They really work—regardless of your profession, talent level, or experience. They improve your performance. A life without any systems is a life where the person must face every task and challenge from scratch.

Think of something you consistently find stressful or overwhelming. Then brain-storm some different systems for yourself that will maximize your time and increase your efficiency in dealing with that issue.

DAY

49

*We may be very busy, we may be very efficient,
but we will also be truly effective only when
we begin with the end in mind.*
STEPHEN COVEY

When I started creating systems for my personal growth, they were very targeted. I knew I would be speaking every week of my life. So I started reading and finding quotes and illustrations that I filed daily. My efforts had to support and advance my abilities in those areas.

People who excel, regardless of their profession, develop systems to help them achieve the big picture. It's not enough to be busy. If you're busy planning, busy reading books, and busy going to conferences, but they aren't targeted on the areas essential to your success, you're not helping yourself. As the saying goes, unhappiness is not knowing what we want and killing ourselves to get it.

What is your big picture? In what areas must you grow to achieve your purpose? Author and professor C. S. Lewis said, "Every person is composed of a few themes." What are yours? And what systems can you develop to advance yourself in those areas today and every day? I had to stop reading books simply for pleasure and read books that would help me in my areas of strength. I also took two speed-reading classes to help me improve. What must you do?

What are your strengths? And what systems can you develop to build on those strengths and help you reach your big-picture goals today and every day?

DAY

50

*Perhaps the very best question you can memorize
and repeat over and over is, "What is the
most valuable use of my time right now?"*
BRIAN TRACY

A system is of limited help to you if it doesn't take into account your priorities. To shape the system you should create for yourself, ask yourself, "When is my most valuable time?" because you'll want to always make the most of it. For me it's mornings. When I recognized that thirty years ago, I stopped scheduling breakfast meetings. Imagine how much of my prime productivity time was spared and utilized.

Making that decision was pretty easy. Others have been more difficult. I am very opportunity driven, and I tend to want to do *everything*. I love saying yes. I have a very hard time saying no. As a result, I get spread too thin. To deal with that, I had to develop a system whereby requests for my time had to go to a group who would decide whether or not I would accept. We fondly named them the Hatchet Committee. Why? Because they put the ax to ninety percent of the requests that came in. It was the best system I could employ to help me maintain my priorities when it came to my time.

What systems do you need to put into place to help you maintain your priorities? And what people do you need to give responsibility and power to so they can help you?

DAY

51

*No plan is worth the paper it is printed on
unless it starts you doing something.*
WILLIAM DANFORTH

If you wanted a new home and had the most beautiful blueprints in the world for the most spectacular house, what value would they have if there was no action plan to build it? Not much. It's not enough just to plan, though planning is important. Both plan and action must go together. The plan creates the track. The action provides the traction. So anytime you have a goal but you think you won't be able to reach it, don't adjust the goal. Adjust the action steps.

People who develop systems that include action steps are almost always more successful than people who don't. Even less talented people with fewer resources accomplish more if they have developed the habit of taking action. That's one of the reasons I've developed the habit of asking myself three questions every time I learn something new: *Where can I use this? When can I use this? Who needs to know this?*

This has become a discipline in my life, so I always have a bias toward action when I learn something new.

Does your system for growth have a built-in bias toward action? What actions steps do you need to maintain to reach your goal?

DAY

52

Measurement is the first step that leads to control and eventually to improvement. If you can't measure something, you can't understand it. If you can't understand it, you can't control it. If you can't control it, you can't improve it.

H. JAMES HARRINGTON

Any kind of progress requires the ability to measure, and for that reason, your growth systems must include a way to measure your results. Measurement enables you to set goals, evaluate progress, judge results, and diagnose problems, which will help stimulate your growth progress.

One effective way to improve your results is to develop systems that employ organization. The number one time waster for most people is looking for things that are lost, which organization can eliminate. And organizing your time is more important than how you spend your money. Money mistakes can be corrected. But once time has passed, it's gone forever.

Being organized gives a sense of power. When you know your purpose and priorities and you have ordered your day, week, or year according to them, you have clarity of thought that strengthens everything you do. You develop an efficiency that helps you to follow through on everything you do. There are few things like it. Make sure your systems make you as organized as you can possibly be.

Write an outline of your system for growth, including a tangible way to measure your results. How does your system help you organize your time?

DAY

53

Every problem introduces a person to himself.
JOHN McDONNELL

How do you usually respond to bad experiences? Do you explode in anger, or shrink into yourself emotionally, or detach yourself from the experience as much as possible, or try ignoring it?

Each time we encounter a painful experience, we get to know ourselves a little better. Pain can stop us dead in our tracks. Or it can cause us to make decisions we would like to put off, deal with issues we would rather not face, and make changes that make us feel uncomfortable. Pain prompts us to face who we are and where we are. What we do with that experience defines who we become.

No matter what you have gone through in your life—or what you are currently going through—you have the opportunity to grow from it. It's sometimes very difficult to see the opportunity in the midst of the pain, but it is there. You must be willing to not only look for it, but also pursue it.

Think of a recent negative experience and write an honest assessment of your attitude toward it. What did you do in response? How might you want to approach such experiences in the future?

DAY

54

*Expecting the world to treat you fairly just because
you're a good person is a little like expecting the bull
not to charge you because you're a vegetarian.*
DENNIS WHOLEY

Most of us want our lives to only be filled with ups. That's not realistic. No matter who you are, where you live, what you do, or what your background is, you will have to deal with downs—with bad experiences.

What separates people who thrive from those who merely survive? I believe it's how they face their problems and whether they use pain as a stepping-stone for success. I've never known anyone who said, "I love problems," but I've known many who have admitted that their greatest gains came through their pain.

Everyone has a pain file. Life's difficulties do not allow us to stay the same. They move us. The question is, in which direction will we be moved: forward or backward? Do we become better or bitter? Will negative experiences and failures limit us or lead us to grow?

Most successful people will point to the hard times in their lives as key points in their journey of development. I've learned to let my painful experiences be a catalyst for my development. Growth is the best possible outcome for any negative experience.

Think of something negative that happened to you recently. Now think about how you can learn from it or create a positive outcome from it. Write about it.

DAY

55

Life is not the way it's supposed to be. It's the way it is.
The way you cope with it is what makes the difference.
VIRGINIA SATIR

You cannot control much of what happens to you in life. However, you can control your attitude. And you can choose to rise above your circumstances and refuse to allow negative experiences to undermine who you are and what you believe. And you can be resolved to find something positive to learn in the face of tragedy.

I have come to adopt a positive life stance because I believe it gives me the best chance to succeed while putting me in the best position to help others succeed. I came to develop this mind-set by way of the following thinking:

Life is filled with good and bad.
Some of the good and bad I can't control—that's life.
Some of the good and bad will find me.
If I have a positive life stance, the good and bad will become better.
If I have a negative life stance, the good and bad will become worse.
Therefore I choose a positive life stance.

If you can maintain a positive life stance, you put yourself in the best position to manage bad experiences and turn them into positive growth.

Utilizing a current negative experience or situation, what new path can you create to maintain a positive life stance to turn it into positive growth?

DAY

Life begins at the end of your comfort zone.
DONALD WALSH

I believe that creativity begins when you're at the end of your rope. When you feel the pain of bad experiences, creativity gives you the opportunity to turn that pain into gain. The secret is to use the energy that comes from either adrenaline or anger or disappointment to creatively solve problems and learn lessons.

When I experienced a heart attack at age fifty-one, the excruciating pain and the belief in that moment that I wasn't going to see my family again made me face the fact that I needed to change the way I was living. It gave me an opportunity to creatively turn my life around. A bend in the road is not the end of the road unless you fail to make the turn.

The next time you find yourself in the midst of a bad experience, remind yourself that you are on the cusp of an opportunity to change and grow. Whether you do will depend on how you react to your experience, and the changes you make as a result. Allow your emotions to be the catalyst for change, think through how to change to make sure you are making good choices, and then take action.

Write down the last three bad experiences you've had, along with what—if anything—you learned from each. Consider whether you decided to make changes based on what you learned and rate yourself on how well you did at implementing those changes in your life.

DAY

57

Not every thing that is faced can be changed.
But nothing can be changed until it is faced.
JAMES BALDWIN

It is nearly impossible to grow in any significant way when you don't take responsibility for yourself and your life. That means that you need to recognize that your circumstances don't define you. They are outside of you and need not negatively impact your values and standards. At the same time, you must take responsibility for your life and the choices you make.

People who overcome bad experiences avoid the label of "victim" and take responsibility for moving forward. They don't say, "What happened to me is the worst thing in the world, and I'll never be free of it." They say, "What happened to me was bad, but other people are worse off, and I won't give up." They do not wallow in self-pity or ask, "Why me?" And that's a good thing, because it's one short step from "why me" to "woe is me."

Train yourself to fight for positive changes. Remember that your choices will lead to either the pain of self-discipline or the pain of regret. I'd rather live with the pain of self-discipline and reap the positive rewards than live with the pain of regret.

What steps will you take today to reap positive rewards rather than the pain of regret for a past bad experience that you have allowed to make you a "victim"?

DAY

58

*Ninety-nine percent of leadership failures
are failures of character.*

NORMAN SCHWARZKOPF

It comes as little surprise that the most admired quality in leaders is honesty. People want to follow leaders of good character. No one likes to work with unreliable people. But before we work with any other person, who do we have to rely on every day? Ourselves! That's why character is so important. If you cannot trust yourself, you won't ever be able to grow. Good character, with honesty and integrity at its core, is essential to success in any area of life. Without it, a person is building on shifting sand.

Most people focus too much on competence and too little on character. How often does a person miss a deadline because he didn't follow through when he should have? How frequently do people fail to grow because they didn't take time to read helpful books but rather spent their time on something less worthwhile? These shortcomings are the result of character, not capacity.

Character growth only happens intentionally, and it determines the height of your personal growth. And without personal growth, you can never reach your potential.

Write an honest review of your character. Can you trust yourself? Is honesty and integrity at the core of your character? What's lacking?

DAY

59

Character is a quality that embodies many important traits such as integrity, courage, perseverance, confidence, and wisdom. . . . Character is something that you create within yourself and must take responsibility for changing.

JIM ROHN

More than twenty-five hundred years ago, the Proverbs writer noted that as we think in our hearts, so we become (Proverbs 23:7). That ancient idea has been both echoed by other wisdom writers and confirmed by modern science. What we believe really matters. We reap what we sow. What we do or neglect to do in the privacy of our daily lives impacts who we are. If you neglect your heart, mind, and soul, it changes who you are on the outside as well as on the inside.

Before you can *do*, you must *be*. The right motions outwardly with wrong motives inwardly will not bring lasting progress. Continual growth and lasting success are the result of aligning the inside and the outside of our lives. And getting the inside right must come first—with solid character traits that provide the foundation for growth.

Write an assessment of where you have put most of your focus on improving your life: on the inside or on the outside? Do you feel you are playing a role rather than being yourself? What do you need to do to change your focus?

DAY

60

*Winning in life is more than just money . . . it's about
winning on the inside . . . and knowing that you have played
the game of life with all you had . . . and then some.*
DOUG FIREBAUGH

We often cannot determine what happens *to* us, but
we can always determine what happens *within* us. For
instance, when we fail to make the right character choices
within us, we give away ownership of ourselves. We
belong to others—to whatever gains control of us. And
that puts us in a bad place. How can you ever reach your
potential and become the person you can be if others are
making your choices for you?

If you want to be successful, you must prioritize building your inside ahead of your outside. The growth of my
own character has come as the result of hard-fought personal choices. They were not easily made and they are not
easily managed. Every day there is a battle from the outside for me to compromise or surrender them. Regretfully,
there have been times when I have. But whenever that's
happened, I have diligently gone after them to return them
to their respectful place . . . inside of me.

In what areas are your poor choices being influenced by other people or things? Describe what you can do in one of those areas to regain ownership of your life. What hard battles will you need to fight to keep growing in that area?

DAY

61

Here is a simple, rule-of-thumb guide for behavior:
Ask yourself what you want people to do for you,
then grab the initiative and do it for them. (MSG)
The Golden Rule

If you had to pick only one guideline for life and building character, you couldn't do better than following the Golden Rule: Do to others what you would have them do to you. It prompts you to focus on other people. It leads you to be empathetic. It encourages you to take the high road. And if you stick to it—especially when it's difficult—you can't help but become the kind of person others want to be around. After all, in the end in all of our relationships we are either plusses or minuses in the lives of others. The Golden Rule helps us to remain a plus.

Another powerful guideline is to build your life on principles. Do you know what they call a speaker who teaches what he doesn't believe? A hypocrite! Borrowed beliefs have no passion, therefore no power. Some of the things I was passionate about thirty years ago, I'm still just as passionate about today. I don't ever want to become one of those individuals who lack principles and passion. I bet you don't want to either.

Are you willing to live by the Golden Rule? What will you do today to serve the people you care about with one hundred percent of your focus?

DAY

62

Humility is the solid foundation of all the virtues.
CONFUCIUS

Humility paves the way for character growth, and that sets us up for personal growth. Andy Stanley says, "I've concluded that while nobody plans to mess up their life, . . . we don't put the necessary safeguards in place to ensure a happy ending." So how do we do that?

The first thing to do is remind ourselves of the big picture. It's said that President John F. Kennedy kept a small plaque in the White House with the inscription "Oh God, thy sea is so great and my boat is so small." If the person known as the leader of the free world can keep perspective of his true place in the world, so should we.

Beyond that, Rick Warren suggests admitting our weaknesses, being patient with others' weaknesses, and being open to correction. To that, I add that we need to be humble, teachable, open to new ideas, and thirsty for knowledge. Then few things are better for cultivating character and developing humility than serving others. Putting others first right-sizes our egos and perspective. And don't forget to maintain an attitude of gratitude to those to whom we are indebted for all we've received.

What safe-guards are you building into your life to keep you humble? Set aside at least an hour every week for helping others, and schedule it today.

DAY

63

*If you want a better world, composed of better nations, . . .
made up of better cities, comprised of better neighborhoods,
illuminated by better churches, populated by better families,
then you'll have to start by becoming a better person.*

TONY EVANS

The final "rung" on my character ladder is the determination to keep building character and living at the highest standard until the day I die. I am endeavoring to do that by doing the right thing and becoming a better person every day. To do the right thing, I don't wait to feel like it. I recognize that emotion follows motion. Do the right thing and you feel right. Do the wrong thing and you feel bad. If you take control of your behavior, your emotions will fall into place.

If we desire to grow and reach our potential, we must pay more attention to our character than to our success. We must recognize that personal growth means more than expanding our minds and adding to our skills. It means increasing our capacity as human beings. It means maintaining core integrity, even when it hurts. It means maturing our souls.

Orison Swett Marden once described a successful person by saying, "He was born mud and died marble." Isn't that a wonderful thought? I hope that can be said of me at the end of my life, and I hope the same for you.

What are you doing every day to develop the habit of character growth? Where do you need to give more attention to maturing your soul?

DAY

64

*The real tragedy is the tragedy of the man who never in his life
braces himself for his one supreme effort, who never stretches
to his full capacity, never stands up to his full stature.*

ARNOLD BENNETT

Most people use only a small fraction of their ability and rarely strive to reach their full potential. There is no tension to grow in their lives, little desire to stretch. Too many people are willing to settle for average in life. I cannot stand the idea of settling for average, can you? Nobody admires average. The best organizations don't pay for average. Mediocrity is not worth shooting for. We must be aware of the gap that stands between us and our potential, and let the tension of that gap motivate us to keep striving to become better.

If you have ever settled for the status quo and then wondered why your life isn't going the way you'd hoped, you need to realize that you will only reach your potential if you have the courage to push yourself outside your comfort zone and break out of a mind-set of mediocrity. You must be willing to leave behind what feels familiar, safe, and secure. You must give up excuses and push forward. You must be willing to face the tension that comes from stretching toward your potential.

In what areas of your life have you lost your stretch and settled in? Where have you accepted being average rather than striving to become better? Write down the reasons why stretching toward your potential is worth the effort.

DAY

65

Your circumstances may be uncongenial, but they shall not long remain so if you but perceive an ideal and strive to reach it. You cannot travel within and stand still without.

JAMES ALLEN

Most people have a dream. For some, it's on the tip of their tongue, and for others, it's buried deep in their hearts, but most everyone has one. However, not very many people are pursuing it. What is stopping them from leaving the job they don't like or losing the weight that is making them unhealthy? For that matter, what is stopping you? Instead of wishing, wanting, and waiting, people need to search inside themselves for reasons to start.

It's wise to remember that our situation in life is mainly due to the choices we make and the actions we do—or fail to—take. If you are merely average or if you are no closer to your dream this year than you were last year, you can choose to accept it, defend it, cover it up, and explain it away. Or you can choose to change it, grow from it, and forge a new path.

You need to measure what you're doing against what you're capable of. If you have no idea what you might be capable of, talk to people who care about you and believe in you. Use that image to inspire you to start stretching.

What goals haven't you hit that you believe you're capable of? What steps will you take to change, grow, and forge a new path?

DAY

66

*Have you ever met a successful person who wasn't restless—
who was satisfied with where he or she was in life?
They want new challenges. They want to get up and go . . .
and that's one of the reasons they're successful.*

Alex Trebek

Growth doesn't come from staying in your comfort zone. You can't improve and avoid change at the same time. Innovation and progress are initiated by people who push for change. So how do I embrace change and kick myself out of my comfort zone?

First of all, I stop looking over my shoulder. It's difficult to focus on your past and change in the present. That's why for years I had on my desk a little plaque that said, "Yesterday ended last night." It helped me to focus on the present and work to improve what I could today.

The second thing I do is work to develop my "reach muscle." The greatest stretching seasons of life come when we do what we have never done, push ourselves harder, and reach in a way that is uncomfortable to us. That takes courage. But the good news is that it causes us to grow in ways we thought were impossible. A. G. Buckham, who pioneered aviation photography in the early days of flight, observed, "Monotony is the awful reward of the careful." If you want to grow and change, you must take risks.

What will you do today to develop your "reach muscle"? What risk must you take to do what you've never done before?

DAY

67

Nature has everywhere written her protest against idleness; everything that ceases to struggle, which remains inactive, rapidly deteriorates. It is the struggle toward an ideal, the constant effort to get higher and further, which develops manhood and character.

JAMES TERRY WHITE

When we stop stretching, I believe we stop really living. We may keep on breathing. Our vital signs may be working. But we are dead on the inside and dead to our greatest possibilities.

I'm getting older. I will not always be able to perform at my peak level. But I intend to keep reading, asking questions, talking to interesting people, working hard, and exposing myself to new experiences until I die. Too many people are dead but just haven't made it official yet! Rabbi Nachman of Bratslav said, "If you won't be better tomorrow than you were today, then what do you need tomorrow for?" The following words sum up how I feel: *I'm not where I'm supposed to be, I'm not what I want to be, but I'm not what I used to be. I haven't learned how to arrive; I've just learned how to keep going.*

I'm going to keep on stretching until I'm all stretched out. And I won't stop when I experience success. I won't allow success to derail my growth.

Write a declaration of commitment to lifelong personal growth and what you will do to safeguard it as you experience successes and failures. Then sign and date it.

DAY

68

To be what we are, and to become what we are capable of becoming, is the only end in life.
ROBERT LOUIS STEVENSON

Mahatma Gandhi stated, "The difference between what we do and what we are capable of doing would suffice to solve most of the world's problems." That difference is the gap between good and great. And what closes the gap is our willingness to stretch and grow.

People who exist on the "good" side of the gap live in the land of the permissible and the okay. Make a decision to cross over the gap and live on the "great" side. That is the land of the possible. It's where people achieve in extraordinary fashion. They do more than they believed they were capable of, and they make an impact. How? By continually focusing on making the next step of growth. They continually leave their comfort zone and stretch toward their capacity zone.

Philosopher Søren Kierkegaard said, "A possibility is a hint from God. One must follow it." That possibility path is God giving us an opportunity to make a difference. As we follow it, we stop asking ourselves what we are, and we start asking what we can become. Significance is birthed within each of us. If we are willing to stretch, that seed can grow until it begins to bear fruit in our lives.

In what areas are you currently living in the land of the okay? What do you need to do to cross over the gap to "great"? What is one stretching step that you can take this week to move from what you are to what you can become?

DAY

69

*People will cling to an unsatisfactory way of life
rather than change in order to get something better
for fear of getting something worse.*
ERIC HOFFER

Life has many intersections, opportunities to go up
or down. At these intersections we make choices. We can
add something to our life, subtract from it, or exchange
something we have for something we don't. Too often,
people make life more difficult for themselves because they
make bad choices at the intersections of their life or they
decline to make choices because of fear. But it's important
to remember that while we don't always get what we want,
we always get what we choose.

Whenever I face an opportunity for a trade-off, I ask
myself: What are the pluses and minuses of this trade-off?
By trying to figure out the pluses and minuses of any given
choice, it helps me deal with the fear that closes me off
from a potential opportunity. Looking at cold, hard facts
has also led me to discover that I have a tendency to over-
estimate the value of what I currently have and underestimate the value of what I may gain by giving it up.

I also ask myself: Will I endure this change or grow
through this change? Positive trade-offs should be seen as
opportunities for growth and seized.

Describe a worthwhile trade-off you made in the past. What lessons did you learn from making that decision that you can continue to use today?

DAY

70

When we are no longer able to change a situation,
we are challenged to change ourselves.

VIKTOR FRANKL

Often I hear people expressing the hope that things will change. At those moments, I want to tell them that the difference between where we are and where we want to be is created by the changes we are willing to make in our lives. When you want something you have never had, you must do something you've never done to get it. Otherwise you keep getting the same results.

Changes to our lives always begin with changes we are willing to make personally. That's often not easy, because to change your life, *you* need to change. We just need to remember that we are the key, that everyone can change, and we will be rewarded when we change.

For many, change is also a real challenge because they don't want to wait for the reward. We want the outcome, but we have to face the end of something we like, and face the uncertainty between that ending and the hoped-for new beginning. The change feels like a loss. The in-between periods of transition require our choice to have a positive attitude and focus on the upcoming benefits of the trade-off.

Is there a trade-off you're considering? Make two lists of pros and cons, one for making the trade, and one for not making it.

DAY

71

Don't fear failure so much that you refuse to try new things.
The saddest summary of life contains three descriptions:
could have, might have, and should have.

LOUIS BOONE

There are many trade-offs in life that can be made at any time. For example, we can give up bad habits to acquire good ones anytime we have the willpower to make the decision. Obviously, the sooner we make such decisions the better, but most of the time they are not time driven.

On the other hand, after some people make a bad trade-off, they panic, feeling that they have blown it and can never recover. But seldom is that true. Most of the time, we can make choices that will help us to come back. So when it comes to choices, never say never. Life is too full of rich possibilities to have that kind of restriction placed upon it.

On other trade-offs, the cycle of change gives us windows of opportunity in which to make decisions. On a few trade-offs that cycle only goes around once. Miss it and the opportunity is gone.

But we cannot hold back in fear. We all have the power of choice, but every time we make a choice, our choice has power over us. It changes us. Even the bad choices can ultimately help us to change for good, because they clarify our thinking and show us ourselves.

Describe a trade-off you made in the past that you regret having made. What lessons did you learn from making that decision that you can continue to use today?

DAY

*Each success only buys an admission ticket
to a more difficult problem.*
HENRY KISSINGER

When most of us are starting out in life, we have little to give up and are highly motivated to change. But as we climb and accumulate some of the good things of life, the trade-offs demand a higher price and we're less inclined to change because we don't have to.

One of the dangers of success is that it can make a person unteachable. Many people become convinced that they know enough to succeed, discontinue their growth, and begin to coast. They trade innovation and growth for a formula, which they follow time after time. "You can't argue with success," they say. But they're wrong. Why? Because the skills that got you here are probably not the skills that will get you there. This is especially true today when everything is changing quickly. Consider that a few years ago neither Twitter nor the iPhone even existed.

No matter how successful you have been up to this point, you can never "stand pat." If you want to keep growing and learning, you need to keep making trades. And they will cost you.

How are your successes impacting your willingness to make trade-offs and take risks? What will you do to remain innovative and growing?

DAY

73

*The only job security we have is our individual
commitment to personal development.*
KEVIN TURNER

I have come to see making trade-offs as a way of
life. But not everything in my life is on the trading block.
I'm not willing to trade my marriage for my career, or
my relationship with my children or grandchildren for
fame or fortune. And I'm not willing to trade away my
values for anything or anyone. These kinds of trade-offs
only lead to regret. And they are difficult to recover from.
That's why I believe it's important to create systems and
draw lines to keep ourselves safe.

What kinds of trade-offs have you been making so
far in your life? Have you thought about it? Have you
developed guidelines to help you decide what to strive for
and what to give up in return?

One of my personal trade-off guidelines is that I am
willing to give up financial security for potential tomorrow. I've made seven major career moves in my lifetime, and in five of them, I took a pay cut to do so. Why?
Because I value opportunity over security. And I knew I
would work hard and be able to earn the ability to make
more money in the long run.

Write your own personal list of trade-off principles. What guidelines help you decide what to strive for and what to give up in return?

DAY

74

He who would accomplish little must sacrifice little;
he who would achieve much must sacrifice much.
JAMES ALLEN

Allow me to give you four additional trade-offs that I have thought through that may help you to develop your own guidelines:

I am willing to give up immediate gratification for personal growth. When it comes to growth and success, immediate gratification is almost always the enemy of growth. We can choose to please ourselves and plateau, or we can delay our gratification and grow.

I am willing to give up the fast life for the good life. What is the good life? Richard J. Leider and David A. Shapiro say it is "Living in the Place you belong, with the people you Love, doing the Right Work, on Purpose."

I am willing to give up security for significance. The great men and women of history were not great because of what they earned and owned, but rather for what they gave their lives to accomplish.

I am willing to give up addition for multiplication. My attitude in the beginning was, "What can I do *for* others?" But that is addition. Once I began to learn about leadership, my question changed to, "What can I do *with* others?" That's multiplication.

What trade do you need to make right now that you have been unwilling to make? Applying your guidelines, what step will you take to make that decision?

DAY

75

In spite of illness, in spite even of the archenemy sorrow, one can remain alive long past the usual date of disintegration if one is unafraid of change, insatiable in intellectual curiosity, interested in big things, and happy in small ways.

ƎDITH WHARTON

I believe curiosity is the key to being a lifelong learner, and if you want to keep growing, you must keep on learning. Curious people are interested in life, people, ideas, experiences, and events, and they live in a constant state of wanting to learn more. They continually ask *why?*

Curiosity is the primary catalyst for self-motivated learning. People who remain curious don't need to be encouraged to ask questions or explore. They just do it—all the time. And they keep doing it. They know that the trail to discovery is just as exciting as the discoveries themselves, because there are wonderful things to be learned along the way.

Curiosity helps a person to think and expand possibilities beyond the ordinary. Asking *why?* fires the imagination. It leads to discovery. It opens up options. It takes people beyond the ordinary and leads to extraordinary living. People say not to cross a bridge until you come to it, but as someone once said, "This world is owned by people who have crossed bridges in their imagination before anyone else has."

Do you consider yourself a curious person? What triggers your curiosity and learning development? What can you do to expand that?

DAY

76

Some men see things as they are and ask why.
Others dream things that never were and ask why not.
GEORGE BERNARD SHAW

Many people fail to reach their potential—not because they lack capacity but because they are unwilling to expand their beliefs and break new ground. But here's the good news: You can change your thinking and as a result, your life. Give yourself permission to be curious. The single greatest difference between a curious, growing person and those who aren't is the belief that you can learn, grow, and change. You must go after growth. Knowledge, understanding, and wisdom will not seek you out. You must go out and acquire it. The best way to do that is to remain curious.

The way to approach life and learning is to have a beginner's mind-set, which means wondering why and asking a lot of questions until you get answers. It also means being open and vulnerable. If your attitude is like that of a beginner, you have no image to uphold and your desire to learn more is stronger than the desire to look good. Yes, you will at times look foolish. Most people don't like that. Do you know what my response is? Get over yourself! Richard Thalheimer says, "Curb your ego and keep asking questions."

What can you do to maintain a beginner's mind-set? What new challenge can you attempt that will make you feel your inexperience? Or if you have come to think of yourself as an expert, how can you change your mind-set to become an open learner in that area?

DAY

77

Never lose a holy curiosity.
ALBERT EINSTEIN

The secret to maintaining Einstein's "holy curiosity" is to always keep asking *why?* Scientist and philosopher Georg Christoph Lichtenberg observed, "One's first step in wisdom is to question everything—and one's last is to come to terms with everything." Those are the bookends for continuous growth. Ask why. Explore. Evaluate what you discover. Repeat. That's a pretty good formula for growth. Never forget, anyone who knows all the answers is not asking the right questions.

Neither educational institutions nor the corporate world typically stimulate creative thought and growth. To find it, you must seek out other curious people. Being around people with great curiosity is contagious. I know of few better ways of cultivating and sustaining curiosity.

Another way to remain curious is to begin each day with a determination to learn something new, experience something different, or meet someone you don't already know. See each day as having multiple opportunities to learn, maintain a sensitivity and awareness that opens you up to new experiences, and take time at the end of the day to ask yourself questions that prompt you to think about what you learned.

Make a list of the people you spend the most time with and rate each person on his or her level of curiosity and creativity. Do you need to make some intentional changes to spend time with more curious people?

DAY

78

Almost every advance in art, cooking, medicine, agriculture, engineering, marketing, politics, education, and design has occurred when someone challenged the rules and tried another approach.

ROGER VON OECH

Curious, growing people train themselves to see failure as a sign of progress rather than as a sign of weakness. They know that it is impossible to continually try without sometimes failing. It's part of the curiosity journey. Therefore, they make failure their friend. They ask, "Why did this happen? What can I learn? How can I grow from this?" As a result, you fail fast, learn fast, and get to try again fast. That leads to growth and future success.

And if you are dedicated to personal growth, you need to eliminate the mind-set that says, "If it ain't broke, don't fix it." No idea is perfect. No matter how good it is, it can always be improved. I suggest you develop a questioner's mind-set and replace it with these questions:

If it ain't broke, how can we make it better?
If it ain't broke, when is it likely to break in the future?
If it ain't broke, how long will it serve as the world changes?

If you want to avoid growing too comfortable and becoming stagnant, keep challenging the process.

Examine the things you do regularly. In what areas are there better ways of getting things done? Make a list of new ways to achieve the same goals. What improvements can you make today?

DAY

79

There ain't no rules around here!
We're trying to accomplish something!
THOMAS EDISON

I am easily frustrated by people who refuse to think outside of their self-imposed boxes. When someone says, "We've never done it that way before," I want to shake them.

Good ideas are everywhere, but it's hard to see them when you won't look outside of your box. That requires an abundance mind-set. Instead of remaining confined, people need to break down the walls of their boxes, get out, and become hunters of ideas. Most revolutionary ideas were disruptive violations of existing rules. The best way to make a sluggish mind active is to disturb its routine. Getting outside the box leads to growth.

Perhaps the greatest way to remain curious and keep growing is to enjoy life. Tom Peters observed, "The race will go to the curious, the slightly mad, and those with an unsatiated passion for learning and daredeviltry." I believe it honors God when we enjoy life and live it well. That means taking risks—sometimes failing, sometimes succeeding, but always learning. When you enjoy your life, the lines between work and play begin to blur. We do what we love and love what we do. Everything becomes a learning experience.

Spend time today doing something you enjoy. Afterwards, think about why you enjoy that activity. How might you incorporate what you enjoy about it more in other areas of your daily life?

DAY

The cure for boredom is curiosity.
There is no cure for curiosity.
DOROTHY PARKER

When you're curious, the entire world opens up to you and there are few limits on what you can learn and how you can develop. So are you living a curious life? To know the answer, ask yourself:

1. Do you believe you can be curious?
2. Do you have a beginner's mind-set?
3. Have you made *why* your favorite word?
4. Do you spend time with curious people?
5. Do you learn something new every day?
6. Do you partake of the fruit of failure?
7. Have you stopped looking for *the* right answer?
8. Have you gotten over yourself?
9. Do you get out of the box?
10. Are you enjoying your life?

If your answers are yes, you probably are curious. If not, you need to change. And you can. It has everything to do with developing curiosity and a willingness to ask *why?*

Answer the ten questions. If you answer no to a question, explain why. What can you do to change your no to a yes?

DAY

81

Example is not the main thing in influencing others.
It is the only thing.
ALBERT SCHWEITZER

When I first made personal growth my number one priority, I found my first mentors in the pages of books. That is a great place to start, and I am still learning from dozens of people every year whom I will never meet. But I found that if I wanted to become the person I desired to be, I needed to find personal mentors who were ahead of me to learn from. Why? Because it's hard to improve when you have no one but yourself to follow. If you follow only yourself, you will find yourself going in circles.

We become like the people we admire and the models we follow. For that reason, we should take great care when determining which people we ask to mentor us. They must not only display excellence in their area of expertise and possess skill sets from which we can learn; they must also demonstrate character worthy of emulating.

As you look for role models and mentors, scrutinize their personal lives as carefully as their public performance. Your values will be influenced by theirs, so you shouldn't be too casual about whom you choose to follow.

Describe where you are currently in your life and the direction you would like to go. Write a list of the qualities that you need in a good mentor to help take you there.

DAY

82

*As I grow older I pay less attention to what men say.
I just watch what they do.*
ANDREW CARNEGIE

For us to be able to observe models up close and see what they do, we must have some contact with them. That requires access and availability. For us to be actively mentored, we must have time with people to watch their actions, ask questions, and learn from their answers.

The greatest piece of advice I can give in the area of availability is that when you are looking for a mentor, don't shoot too high too soon. If you are a high school student learning to play the cello, you don't need to be mentored by Yo-Yo Ma. If you're just starting out, nearly all of your questions can be answered by someone two or three levels ahead of you (not ten). And their answers will be fresh because they will have recently dealt with the issues you're dealing with. Spend the majority of your time being mentored by people who are available, willing, and suited for the stage you are on. And as you progress in your development, find new mentors for your new level of growth.

Try to identify three people who are one or two levels ahead of you in the area where you most want to grow. Write out questions for a specific problem you're dealing with, and try to get time with one of them to ask your questions.

DAY

To know the road ahead, ask those coming back.
CHINESE PROVERB

The farther you go in the pursuit of your potential, the more new ground you will have to break. How do you figure out how to proceed? Benefit from others' experience. Every time I've entered into a new venture, I've sought the advice of people with proven experience. I don't know of a successful person who hasn't learned from more experienced people. Sometimes they follow in their footsteps. Other times they use their advice to help them break new ground. Former New York City mayor Rudy Giuliani says, "All leaders are influenced by those they admire. Reading about them and studying their traits inevitably allows an aspiring leader to develop his own leadership traits."

Good mentors possess wisdom. Their understanding, experience, and knowledge help us to solve problems that we would have a hard time handling on our own. Wise people often use just a few words to help us learn and develop. They open our eyes to worlds we might not have otherwise seen without their help. They help us navigate difficult situations. They help us to see opportunities we would otherwise miss. They make us wiser than our years and experience.

When was the last time you read a book about someone you greatly admire in your field? Search for a biography of someone's life from whom you can learn, then take notes on what you discover.

DAY

84

Great things happen whenever we stop seeing ourselves as God's gift to others, and begin seeing others as God's gift to us.
JAMES S. VUOCOLO

The first question most followers ask of a mentor is, "Do you care for me?" The reason for this question is obvious. Good mentors provide friendship and support, unselfishly working to help you reach your potential. Selfish people will assist you only insofar as it advances their own agenda, and the relationship will always fall short of your expectations. Knowledge without support is sterile. Advice without friendship feels cold. Candor without care is harsh. However, when you are being helped by someone who cares for you, it is emotionally satisfying. Growth comes from both the head and the heart. Only supportive people are willing to share both with you.

A good mentor is a coach who makes a difference in people's lives. They help them grow. They improve their potential. They increase their productivity. They are essential to helping people effect positive change. As I look back over my life, I recognize that the greatest assets of my growth journey were people. No matter who you are, what you have accomplished, how low or how high your life has taken you, you can benefit from having a mentor. If you've never had one, you have no idea how much it can improve your life.

Create a list of long-term models who can give you advice regarding the big picture of your life, in areas such as marriage, parenting, spiritual growth, personal disciplines, career, hobbies, and so on. Who will you approach first about their willingness to mentor you?

DAY

85

The potential that exists within us is limitless and largely untapped . . . when you think of limits, you create them.
ROBERT J. KRIEGEL AND LOUIS PATLER

I've heard that most experts believe people typically use only 10 percent of their true potential. That statement is staggering! If that is true, the average person has huge capacity for improvement. So how do we tap into the unused 90 percent? The answer is found in changing how we think and what we do.

To increase your capacity, stop thinking *more work* and start thinking *what works?* More work will not necessarily increase your capacity. Early in my career, I realized that though I worked hard and kept it up for long hours, I was doing a lot of things instead of the right things. I looked at everything I was doing and started to ask myself, "What works?" That's what I recommend you do. Figure out what works. To do that, ask yourself the following three questions:

What am I required to do?
What gives the greatest return?
What gives me the greatest reward?

These questions will help you to focus your attention on what you must do, what you ought to do, and what you really want to do.

Utilizing the three questions in today's reading, write an effectiveness audit to show whether your thinking is "What works?" instead of "More work."

DAY

86

What would you attempt if you knew you couldn't fail?
Robert Schuller

Another way to increase your capacity for growth is to stop thinking *Can I?* and start thinking *How can I?*

Can I? is a question filled with hesitation and doubt and imposes limitations. If that is the question you regularly ask yourself, you're undermining your efforts before you even begin. When you ask yourself "How can I?" you give yourself a fighting chance to achieve something. The most common reason people don't overcome the odds is that they don't challenge them enough. They don't test their limits. They don't push their capacity.

How can I? assumes there is a way. You just need to find it.

If you have spent time in a negative environment or you have experienced abuse in your life, you may instead need to change your thinking from *I can't!* to *How can I?* I believe every person has the potential to grow, expand, and achieve. The first step in doing that is believing that you can; the second is perseverance. You can change your thinking. You can believe in your potential. As you get started, it may not look like you're making progress. That doesn't matter. Don't give up.

*If you knew you
could not fail
and you had
no limitations,
what would
you attempt?
What is your
gut-level
response to
your answer?
What must you
do to make
the attempt?*

DAY

87

Man's mind, once stretched by a new idea, never regains its original dimensions.

OLIVER WENDELL HOLMES

When it comes to growth, don't stake your future on one "door." It may not open! Consider many possibilities and look for multiple answers to all of your questions.

As I have learned to think in terms of many doors and explore options, here is what I have learned:

> *There is more than one way to do something successfully.*
> *The odds of arriving anywhere increase with creativity and adaptability.*
> *Movement with intentionality creates possibilities.*
> *Failures and setbacks can be great tools for learning.*
> *Knowing the future is difficult; controlling the future is impossible.*
> *Knowing today is essential; controlling today is possible.*
> *Success is a result of continued action filled with continual adjustments.*

The greatest challenge you will ever face is that of expanding your mind. You must be willing to enter uncharted territory, to face the unknown, to conquer your own doubts and fears. But here's the good news. If you can change your thinking, you can change your life.

Brainstorm as many possible "doors" to growth and success as you can. Don't allow yourself to dismiss ideas while you write. Just record them. You may surprise yourself by finding a great idea that changes your future.

DAY

88

*I am always doing that which I cannot do,
in order to learn how to do it.*
PABLO PICASSO

If you want to expand your potential and therefore your capacity, first change your thinking. However, if you change only your thinking and you neglect to change your actions, you will fall far short of your potential.

To start expanding your capacity, stop doing only those things you have done before and start doing those additional worthy things you discover you *could* and *should* do. Doing new things leads to innovation and new discoveries, and among those discoveries is the realization of things you *should* do on a consistent basis. If you do those, you will continue to grow and expand your potential. If you don't, you will plateau.

The process of expanding one's potential is ongoing. It ebbs and flows. Opportunities come and go. The standards we must set for ourselves are constantly changing. What we *could* do changes as we develop. What we *should* do also evolves. We must leave behind some old things to take on new ones. The process of adaptation and expansion never stops. It can be difficult work, leaving our comfort zones and making mistakes to expand, but if we are willing, our lives are changed.

What's working for you? What isn't working? What are you doing too much of, either because you're not being efficient enough or because the activity is off purpose? What changes do you need to make to expand your capacity?

DAY

89

*Going far beyond that call of duty, doing more than others
expect, this is what excellence is all about! And it comes from
striving, maintaining the highest standards, looking after the
smallest detail, and going the extra mile. Excellence means
doing your very best. In everything! In every way.*

JACK JOHNSON

We live in a culture where many people think they are
doing well if they just do what is expected of them. I don't
believe that helps people reach their potential or expand
their capacity. To do that, a person has to do more. Jack
Welch calls this "getting out of the pile."

To distinguish yourself, get noticed, and advance
your career, you need to do and be more. You have to rise
above average. You can do this by asking more of yourself
than others ask, expecting more from yourself than others
expect, believing more in yourself than others believe,
doing more than others think you should have to do, giving
more than others think you should give, and helping more
than others think you should help.

Doing more than is expected does more than just sepa-
rate you from your colleagues by earning you a reputation for
performance. It also trains you to develop a habit for excellence. And that compounds over time. Continued excellence
expands your capabilities and your potential.

Write a description of what you think excellence should look like in your life. Commit yourself to making it happen, and sign and date it.

DAY

90

*If one advances confidently in the direction of his dreams,
and endeavors to live the life which he has imagined, he
will meet with a success unexpected in common hours.*

HENRY DAVID THOREAU

I believe advancing confidently in the direction of one's dreams means doing what is important every day. To do what's not important merely uses up your time. To do the right thing only occasionally does not lead to consistent growth and the expansion of your life. Both components are necessary. Daily growth leads to personal expansion.

Poet Henry Wadsworth Longfellow compared his growth to that of an apple tree. He said, "The purpose of that apple tree is to grow a little new wood each year. That is what I plan to do." He also expressed a similar thought in one of his poems when he wrote, *Not enjoyment and not sorrow is our destined end always; but to live that each tomorrow finds us further than today.*

If we do what's important every day, that can be true for us. You have the potential to keep making progress until the day you die—if you have the right attitude about growth. You need to believe what Rabbi Samuel M. Silver did. "The greatest of all miracles," he said, "is that we need not be tomorrow what we are today, but we can improve if we make use of the potentials implanted in us by God."

Now that you've spent 90 days intensely working on growing, look ahead. Create a list of growth goals that you would like to accomplish in the next year. Make sure the list is attainable but will also require you to stretch. Then identify the goal you want to accomplish in the next 90 days and outline the daily discipline required for you to achieve it.

Look for the next book in the JumpStart series

What is the number one difference between successful people and average people? The way they think. Expand your potential and develop the thinking habits of successful people with this 90-day improvement plan by #1 *New York Times* bestselling author John C. Maxwell. Using a format that makes it easy for you to grow, Maxwell delivers daily inspiration and practical advice to help you maximize the power of your thoughts and achieve your goals. Including engaging lessons, thought-provoking questions, inspiring quotes, and journaling space to track your progress, this portable guide offers everything you need to become a better thinker and experience personal growth in just three short months.

Coming in fall 2015 from Center Street
wherever books are sold.

CENTER
STREET

NEW YORK · BOSTON · NASHVILLE

Introducing the JumpStart Series Community on Facebook

Find other fans of the JumpStart series and maximize your personal and professional growth.

- Interact with other like-minded leaders.
- Receive and share inspiring quotes with your friends.
- Engage with thought-provoking questions and answers.
- Get the latest news about upcoming books in the JumpStart series and receive exclusive information.
- Experience a daily community where you can get ideas on how to apply what you learn.

Visit www.facebook.com/TheJumpStartSeries
and Like the page to get started.

EQUIP mobilizes Christian leaders to transform their world.

Join the movement!

EQUIP®

www.iEQUIP.org

EQUIP Leadership

@EQUIPleaders

THE JOHN MAXWELL COMPANY

Develop Your Self. Build Your Team.

WE INSPIRE, CHALLENGE AND EQUIP LEADERS TO LIVE OUT LEADERSHIP.
HERE'S HOW WE CAN HELP YOU:

ASSESSMENTS Receive valuable feedback that will impact your journey to become a highly effective leader.

TRAINING Become a better team leader or successful mentor by diving into our programs and specialized training.

COACHING Connect with experienced leadership coaches who understand your challenges and support your growth.

RESOURCES Equip yourself and your team with one of over 900 resources that best fits your leadership interests.

EVENTS Take your leadership development to the next level at one of our live experiences.

For more information on how we can serve you, visit WWW.JOHNMAXWELL.COM.
To read John's latest thoughts on leadership, visit WWW.JOHNMAXWELL.COM/BLOG.

The JOHN MAXWELL Co.